The Quotable Fisherman

The Quotable Fisherman

COMPILED AND INTRODUCED BY
NICK LYONS

Illustrations by
Alan James Robinson

SKYHORSE PUBLISHING

Books by Nick Lyons

The Seasonable Angler
Jones Very: Selected Poems (editor)
Fisherman's Bounty (editor)
The Sony Vision
Locked Jaws
Fishing Widows
Two Fish Tales
Bright Rivers
Confessions of a Fly-Fishing Addict
Trout River (text for photographs by Larry Madison)
Spring Creek
A Flyfisher's World
My Secret Fish-Book Life
Sphinx Mountain and Brown Trout
In Praise of Wild Trout (editor)
Hemingway's Many Hearted Fox River
The Quotable Fisherman (editor)

Skyhorse Publishing books may be purchased in bulk at special discounts for sales promotion, corporate gifts, fund-raising, or educational purposes. Special editions can also be created to specifications. For details, contact the Special Sales Department, Skyhorse Publishing, 555 Eighth Avenue, Suite 903, New York, NY 10018 or info@skyhorsepublishing.com.

www.skyhorsepublishing.com

10 9 8 7 6 5 4 3 2 1

Library of Congress Cataloging-in-Publication Data

The quotable fisherman / compiled and introduced by Nick Lyons.
    p. cm.
  Includes bibliographical references and index.
  ISBN 978-1-61608-103-4 (hardcover : alk. paper)
  1. Fishing--Quotations, maxims, etc. I. Lyons, Nick.
  PN6084.F47Q68 2010
  799.1--dc22

                                2010021698

Printed in China

For
LARA

Acknowledgements

My warm thanks to my good friends Ted Leeson, Darrel Martin, and Lamar Underwood for suggesting some of the most memorable quotations in this compilation.

Alan James Robinson's fine linework has given me great pleasure for twenty years and it is a delight to include so much of it now in *The Quotable Fisherman*, making the verbal world of fishing so visually alive.

Christina Rudofsky did a stellar job transcribing and correcting my often scribbled notes.

And my special thanks to my son Tony for insisting that I put together this little book and for being such a firm colleague during challenging days.

Contents

Some of the best fishing is done not in water but in print.

SPARSE GREY HACKLE

I know there are some things I've read that come to mind more often while I'm fishing than anything I can remember that anybody said beside me on stream or pond.

ARNOLD GINGRICH
THE FISHING IN PRINT (1974)

The literature of angling falls into two genres: the instructional and the devotional. The former is written by fishermen who write, the latter by writers who fish.

WILLIAM HUMPHREY
MY MOBY DICK (1978)

Over the years, whenever I've felt that little twinkle in the hairs on the back of my neck, as I encountered an original thought or observation in a fishing book, I've turned the corner of the page down.

ARNOLD GINGRICH
THE FISHING IN PRINT (1974)

The number and excellence of books devoted to the exposition of Angling are so great that no other sport can compare with it in these respects.

JAMES ROBB
NOTABLE ANGLING LITERATURE (1947)

Fishing books, lit by emotion recollected in tranquility, are like poetry . . . We do not think of them as books but as men. They are our companions and not only riverside. Summer and winter they are with us and what a pleasant company they are.

ARTHUR RANSOME
THE FISHERMAN'S LIBRARY (1959)

Foreword

Thoreau, in *Walden*, says, "The wildness and adventure that are in fishing still recommend it to me." After more than seventy years of passionate angling, the wildness and adventure I first felt as a boy of seven or eight fishing a mountain lake are still very much with me. I tremble a little, every time I come near water . . . even puddles. But to those qualities have been added stillness, humor, mystery, friendship, curiosity, discipline, craft, a portal into the natural world, a love of all that strange and dramatic world under water, and so much more. These comments by a wide range of folks who have written about fishing have caught some of the endless diversity I have found in fishing.

From my earliest years, I have been fascinated by what happens beneath the agitated bobber, and what has been said about it all in print. A literary friend once told me that there is no literature of angling whatsoever. I see no need to put it all into a category, nor to rank it or rate it. The words of fishing have given me (and thousands of others) immense pleasure to read; they have lasted through the ages remarkably well; and they often hold much that speaks of matters far beyond the waters, but about the human heart and eye, and the ways of human beings and their passions.

Though most of the quotations here have come from note-books I kept, some have come from a deliberate search for half-remembered passages; and others, often the best, have come from good friends who have shared with me their favorites. Some quotations are contradictory—and why not, for isn't fishing a happy form of play in which speculation and dispute and diversity are every bit as important as surety? Why did that fish take? Why not? Does the body color of a fly or lure matter? The fact that we don't know what the fish will do on a given day leads to such divergent theories—and to part of our sweetest pleasure.

My criteria, like my selection, have been rather arbitrary. I leaned toward what I liked, what interested me, and then tried to make some order of it. There are sections on beginnings, on species, on the nature of a fisherman's passion—on the nature of the pursuit and the natures of those who pursue. There are comments about technical and ethical matters—and some harsh words from a few folks, like Lord Byron, who despised the entire pursuit. I chose passages for a number of reasons: a turn of phrase, a glint of truth, some wit, some wisdom, some practical knowledge. Most are short. Many lack context. Always they lack the whole truth in which they lived as small part. Some are old, some new, a few are overheard or secondhand; but most are from the primary sources, where I found them. From aphoristic writers like Arthur Ransome, one could fill an entire book of this sort; from others, one takes equal or even greater pleasure but remembers, perhaps, fewer specific words. I might have put a few hundred more quotes into this book and even they would have been too few. Now, looking at my selection, I can think of scores of others I might have included, dozens of fine writers not here at all. This is not a clear and scientific process, building such a book; it is biased by its collector, limited by publishing demands, inevitably arbitrary.

Ultimately, these are not the few hundred quotations that I think are the best, or even my absolute favorites. They are a start, is all—a window into the vast and (to me) endlessly fertile world of words about fishing. I hope they cover the full span of a fisherman's life—from the days most passionate fishermen are first hooked to the days of reflection, memoir, philosophy. No "fishing in print" can ever take the place of time on the water—but it adds to the pleasure of the thing itself.

I hope these words are fun to live with, even a bit revealing and wise at times. Even more, I hope they send you to the works from which they've come.

—Nick Lyons
Spring 2010

The Quotable Fisherman

Chapter 1

Beginnings

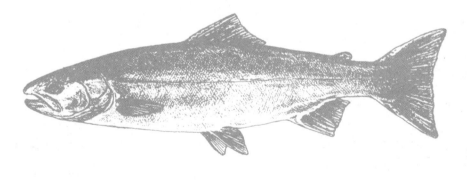

Angling is somewhat like poetry, men are to be born so . . .

> IZAAK WALTON
> *THE COMPLEAT ANGLER* (1653)

Fishing simply sent me out of my mind. I could neither think nor talk of anything else, so that mother was angry and said that she would not let me fish again because I might fall ill from such excitement.

> SERGEI AKSAKOV (1791–1859)
> "MEMOIR"
> TRANSLATED BY ARTHUR RANSOME

It began for me with the capture of a catfish—the most personable and handsome catfish—in the black pool below Poskin's dam.

> BEN HUR LAMPMAN
> *A LEAF FROM FRENCH EDDY* (1965)

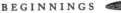

A cork bobs, a stick jerks up, and a fiery stickleback bristling, streaming, describes an unaccustomed arc through the air.

BRIAN CLARKE
THE PURSUIT OF THE STILLWATER TROUT (1975)

To the fisherman born there is nothing so provoking of curiosity as a fishing rod in a case.

ROLAND PERTWEE
"THE RIVER GOD" (1928)

———

"What do you want to do this afternoon, old man?" he asked.

"Fish," I said.

"But you can't always fish," he said.

I told him I could and I was right and have proved it for thirty years and more.

"Well, well," he said, "please yourself, but isn't it dull not catching anything?"

And I said, as I've said a thousand times since, "As if it could be."

ROLAND PERTWEE
"THE RIVER GOD" (1928)

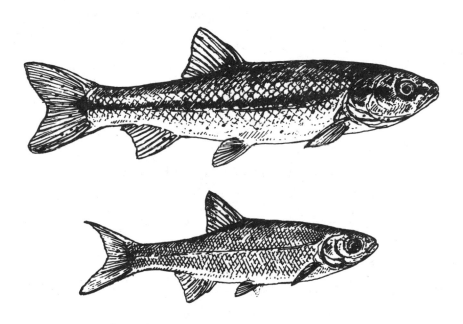

Young anglers love new rivers the way they love the rest of their lives. Time doesn't seem to be of the essence and somewhere in the system is what they are looking for.

THOMAS MCGUANE
"MIDSTREAM"
AN OUTSIDE CHANCE (1990)

I don't WANT to catch a fish, I felt like shouting. I *can't*. I am a prisoner hemmed in by walls of trees and branches. The long rod does not *want* to work in these conditions. I am hot and I look absurd.

MARGOT PAGE
LITTLE RIVERS (1995)

My father was very sure about certain matters pertaining to the universe. To him, all good things—trout as well as eternal salvation—come by grace and grace comes by art and art does not come easy.

NORMAN MACLEAN
A RIVER RUNS THROUGH IT (1976)

I reacted to Mom's dilemma as a boatman with the strong thought forming in my young mind, "It's better to be the fisherman than the rower."

JOAN WULFF
FLY CASTING TECHNIQUES (1987)

. . . perhaps the greatest satisfaction on the first day of the season is the knowledge in the evening that the whole of the rest of the season is to come.

ARTHUR RANSOME
"THE FIRST DAY AT THE RIVER"
ROD AND LINE (1929)

It was late in April, with the river running fine and as clear as a young parson's conscience.

TOM SUTCLIFFE, M.D.
REFLECTIONS ON FISHING (1990)

An old phrase evokes the fly-fisher's spring: the sweet of the year.

R. PALMER BAKER
THE SWEET OF THE YEAR (1965)

I fished a little while ago with a man, not in his first youth, who had wasted the flower of his life on business and golf and gardening and motoring and marriage, and had in this way postponed his initiation far too long.

ARTHUR RANSOME
"ON GIVING ADVICE TO BEGINNERS"
ROD AND LINE (1929)

If a new man is particularly attentive he can learn to fly fish in a half hour. But then he will go on learning as long as he fishes for trout.

ARTHUR R. MACDOUGALL JR.
"RODS AND RODS"
THE TROUT FISHERMAN'S BEDSIDE BOOK (1963)

The true fisherman approaches the first day of fishing with all the sense of wonder and awe of a child approaching Christmas.

ROBERT TRAVER
TROUT MADNESS (1960)

Chapter 2

Fish and
Their World

A trout river is like a book: some parts are dull and some are lively.

> H. G. TAPPLY
> *THE SPORTSMAN'S NOTEBOOK* (1964)

An undisturbed river is as perfect as we will ever know, every refractive slide of cold water a glimpse of eternity.

> THOMAS MCGUANE
> "MIDSTREAM"
> *AN OUTSIDE CHANCE* (1990)

. . . when the lawyer is swallowed up with business and the statesman is preventing or contriving plots, then we sit on cowslip-banks, hear the birds sing, and possess ourselves in as much quietness as these silent silver streams . . .

> IZAAK WALTON
> *THE COMPLEAT ANGLER* (1653)

The stream keeps me from getting lost, and anytime I feel like being a fisherman again, the trout are there, sages themselves, the wise *roshi* that caught me by the way and taught me to love wildness.

CHRISTOPHER CAMUTO
"CAUGHT BY THE WAY"
IN PRAISE OF WILD TROUT (1998)

No angler merely watches nature in a passive way. He enters into its very existence.

JOHN BAILEY
REFLECTIONS ON THE WATER'S EDGE (N.D.)

Greedy little minds are ever busy turning landscapes into slag heaps, housing tracts, canals, freeways and shopping malls, a perversion they zealously pursue under the ragged banner of progress.

SHERIDAN ANDERSON
THE CURTIS CREEK MANIFESTO (1978)

In 1918 I realized that the growing use of the automobile, with its easy transportation, would soon spoil all public trout fishing . . .

EDWARD R. HEWITT
A TROUT AND SALMON FISHERMAN FOR SEVENTY-FIVE YEARS (1948)

. . . knowing a river intimately is a very large part of the joy of fly fishing.

RODERICK L. HAIG-BROWN
A RIVER NEVER SLEEPS (1946)

The San Juan: A river in danger of being loved to death for all the right reasons.

STEVEN J. MEYERS
SAN JUAN RIVER CHRONICLE (1994)

. . . there are enough miles of bright water in the Blue Ridge to support the fly fisherman's deep-seated need to believe in infinite possibilities.

CHRISTOPHER CAMUTO
A FLY FISHERMAN'S BLUE RIDGE (1990)

$E=\frac{1}{2}mv^2$
Fortunately this is translatable. It means: If a trout doubles the speed with which he darts up at a fly, he is putting out four times the amount of energy.

J. W. DUNNE
SUNSHINE AND THE DRY FLY (1924)

The Campbell I know almost as a man should know a river.

RODERICK L. HAIG-BROWN
A RIVER NEVER SLEEPS (1946)

I am a Brother of the Angle, and therefore an enemy to the otter . . .

IZAAK WALTON
THE COMPLEAT ANGLER (1653)

Stalking along from log to log, or plunging their long legs in the oozy swamp, [two large herons] paid no attention to my presence, but occupied themselves with their own fishing arrangements, as if their wilderness were their own.

W. C. PRIME
I GO A-FISHING (1873)

Mother Nature is not fooled by technological fixes.

ROBERT BEHNKE
"WILD TROUT AND NATIVE TROUT—IS THERE A DIFFERENCE?"
IN PRAISE OF WILD TROUT (1998)

As I peered over the bank a good trout backed like a phantom into obscurity.

ROMILLY FEDDEN
GOLDEN DAYS (1919)

Fly-fishers fail in preparing their bait so as to make it alluring in the right quarter, for want of a due acquaintance with the subjectivity of fishes.

GEORGE ELIOT
THE MILL ON THE FLOSS (1860)

He had been hooked two or three times and was consequently as wary as a miser, when his son begins to beat about the bush, introductory to some pecuniary hint.

HEWITT WHEATLY
THE ROD AND LINE (1847)

The existence of such omniscient giants as he, sentient in the deeps of a great pool, gives glamour to a stream and to all the fishing upon it.

HOWARD T. WALDEN II
UPSTREAM AND DOWN (1938)

Every day I see the head of the largest trout I ever hooked, but did not land.

THEODORE GORDON (1914)

Yet fish there be, that
   neither hook nor line

Nor snare, nor net, nor
   engine can make thine.

JOHN BUNYAN
PILGRIM'S PROGRESS (1678)

With the right conditions, Nature herself provides the best and the cheapest way of producing trout, and will produce as many as the food in the river will support.

DERMOT WILSON
FISHING THE DRY FLY (1970)

. . . a gut-shot landscape is no place for wild trout.

TOM PALMER
"TROUT HABITAT IN THE BLACKFOOT COUNTRY"
IN PRAISE OF WILD TROUT (1998)

When you are next complaining about the selectivity of trout, bear the thought in mind: were it not for this fortunate trait, how long would our stream fishing last?

ART FLICK
ART FLICK'S STREAMSIDE GUIDE (1947)

Chapter 3

A Mixed Bag

To me, bream on a fly rod are as pretty fishing as a man can want, but there are times when they aren't worth working for.

JOHN GRAVES
GOODBYE TO A RIVER (1960)

. . . angling—rod and reel, troutline, jugline, grabbling, whatever—offers possibly our last link with the eternal verities of nature and pursuit. And no better fish to pursue than the one with whiskers.

M. H. "DUTCH" SALMON
THE CATFISH AS METAPHOR (1997)

. . . blunt emergence
of bullhead, his slow surge to the bait, glint
of the small, mucusoid eye—
sluggish black spasm of flesh,
he bites, and I haul him out,
but he does not die at once

JOHN ENGELS
"BULLHEAD"
BIG WATER (1995)

I told him a yellow catfish that had looked to weigh
forty pounds had nearly torn the paddle out of my
hands that morning. It was true . . .

JOHN GRAVES
GOODBYE TO A RIVER (1960)

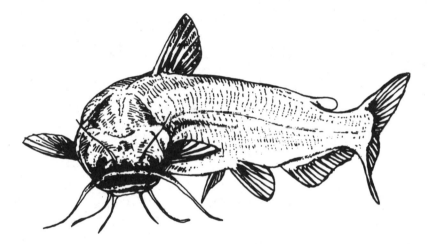

. . . the excitement of a really good night's eel fishing is worthy of compare . . . with the satisfaction derived from howsoever good a day's angling.

J. H. KEENE
THE PRACTICAL FISHERMAN (N.D.)

. . . there are carriers and side-streams on the River Test on which falls of spinners can be so heavy at certain times of the year that the eels have been seen there, lying just beneath the surface and rising to spent flies just as trout do.

PETER LAPSLEY
RIVER TROUT FLYFISHING (1988)

Eels call, on capture, for swift action, firmness of character and a Finnish knife.

ARTHUR RANSOME
"A MIXED BAG"
ROD AND LINE (1929)

Fishing for barbel needs a greater expenditure of worms and faith than I have ever been in a position to afford.

ARTHUR RANSOME
"MY BARBEL"
ROD AND LINE (1929)

No trout, except possibly a very old, very heavy, very wise trout, fights like a large carp.

> STEVEN J. MEYERS
> *SAN JUAN RIVER CHRONICLE* (1994)

A man who fishes habitually for carp has a strange look in his eyes.

> ARTHUR RANSOME
> "CARP"
> *ROD AND LINE* (1929)

You cannot, of course, fish for big carp in half a day. It takes a month.

> H. T. SHERINGHAM
> *COARSE FISHING* (1912)

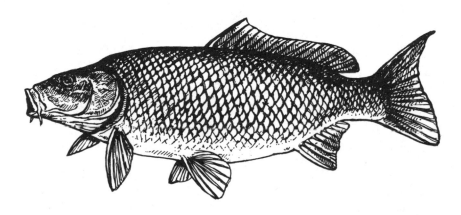

The floating bread-crust works! "Minor tactics" have come to carp fishing.

LESLIE P. THOMPSON
FISHING IN NEW ENGLAND (1955)

Around the kitchen table the family gathers, and following my enthusiastic lead, admire the swelling flanks covered by big shining scales, the symmetrical lines of a body of no mean bulk, and the rather fetching little Mongolian mustaches depending from the sides of a rounded mouth that appears to be on the point of whistling a merry tune.

LESLIE P. THOMPSON
FISHING IN NEW ENGLAND (1955)

The Carp is the queen of rivers—a stately, a good, and a very subtle fish.

IZAAK WALTON
THE COMPLEAT ANGLER (1653)

[The steelhead] can hurtle into the air a split second after he is hooked, and flash hugely out in the murk, like the sword Excalibur thrust up from the depths—at once a gleaming prize and a symbol of battle.

PAUL O'NEIL
"EXCALIBUR: THE STEELHEAD" (1957)

Hunting and fishing are the second and third oldest professions, yet bonefishing is the only sport that I know of, except perhaps swordfishing, that combines hunting and fishing.

STANLEY M. BABSON
BONEFISHING (1965)

I know of no more absorbing adventure than to wade slowly across some white tropic flat. Although the bonefisherman may go home empty-handed, if he has eyes to see and ears to hear he will be a silent observer of the myriads of sea creatures living out their destinies all about him.

STANLEY M. BABSON
BONEFISHING (1965)

All pikes that live long prove to their keepers, because their life is so maintained by the death of so many other fish, even those of his owne kind, which has made him by some writers to be called the tyrant of the rivers, or the freshwater wolf, by reason of his bold, greedy, devouring disposition.

IZAAK WALTON
THE COMPLEAT ANGLER (1653)

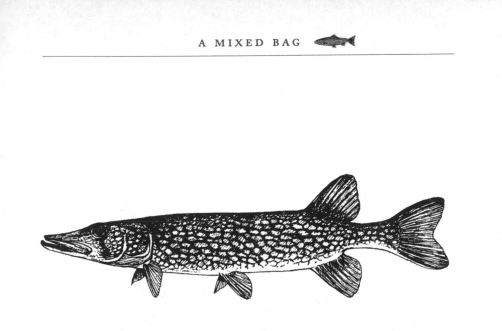

Of the pike:

It is a fish of ambush.

J. H. KEENE
THE PRACTICAL FISHERMAN (N.D.)

Pike

... my friend brought the second partridge to the riverside, tied some big trebles in it and hove it into the air
with his pike rod so that it splashed into the water just
where the other had disappeared. It was gone on the
instant, and my friend landed a twenty-five pounder.

ARTHUR RANSOME
"UNCAUGHT FISH"
ROD AND LINE (1929)

The greediness of pike knows no bounds.

SERGEI AKSAKOV
NOTES ON FISHING (1847)
TRANSLATED BY THOMAS P. HODGE (1997)

... a man going to a pond (where it seems a pike had
devoured all the fish) to water his mule, had a pike bite
his mule by the lips, to which the pike hung so fast, that
the mule drew him out of the water, and by that accident the owner of the mule got the pike ...

IZAAK WALTON
THE COMPLEAT ANGLER (1653)

. . . an organ chorus of red howler monkeys swinging over a jungle stream as the tarpon roll and splash in counterpoint . . .

A. J. MCCLANE
"SONG OF THE ANGLER" (1967)

S: Will I really know when one is on?
F: Will you ever! Blues strike like blacksmiths' hammers.

JOHN HERSEY
BLUES (1987)

. . . blues are both butchers and gluttons. They're cannibals that will eat their young. They will eat anything alive. They have stripped the toes from surfers in Florida . . .

JOHN HERSEY
BLUES (1987)

. . . the big fish, yellow looking in the water, swimming two or three feet under the surface, the huge pectoral fins tucked close to the flanks, the dorsal fin down, the fish looking a round fast-moving log in the water except for the erect curve of that slicing tail.

ERNEST HEMINGWAY
"MARLIN OFF THE MORRO" (1933)

On bass:
This is one of the American freshwater fishes; it is surpassed by none in boldness of biting, in fierce and violent resistance when hooked.

W. H. HERBERT (FRANK FORESTER)
FISHES AND FISHING (1850)

. . . the small-mouth is probably more active in its movements, the large-mouth is more powerful.

JAMES HENSHALL
BOOK OF THE BLACK BASS (1881)

I consider him, inch for inch and pound for pound, the gamest fish that swims.

JAMES HENSHALL
BOOK OF THE BLACK BASS (1881)

Anyone who knows fish knows that pound for pound any salt-water fish is far stronger, far more disinclined to be hauled in on a line than a comparable fresh-water fish.

LOUIS D. RUBIN JR.
THE EVEN-TEMPERED ANGLER (1983)

. . . bluegills . . . ounce for ounce, there is no better scrapper in fresh water.

ELMER RANSOM
FISHING'S JUST LUCK (1945)

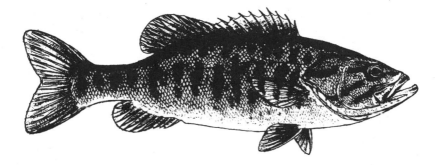

. . . an important attribute in shoreline fishing for large-mouths is a sensitive eye for the slight irregularities which are all that a bass needs to achieve concealment.

HAROLD BLAISDELL
THE PHILOSOPHICAL FISHERMAN (1969)

But if the salmon and trout must be classified as elite in this mythical social structure then let the black bass be given permanent status as the working class of American gamefish. He's tough and he knows it. . . . He's a bass sax grumbling get-down blues in the bayou. He's a factory worker, truck driver, wild catter, lumberjack, barroom bouncer, dock walloper, migrant farmhand, and bear wrassler. And if it's a fight you're looking for, he'll oblige anytime, anywhere. Whether it's a backwater at noon, a swamp at midnight, or dockside at dawn, he'll be there waiting. He's a fierce-eyed, foul-mouthed, tobacco-chewing redneck who has traveled to every corner of the nation, paying his way and giving no quarter.

PAT SMITH
"OLD IRON JAW"
LAMAR UNDERWOOD'S BASS ALMANAC (1979)

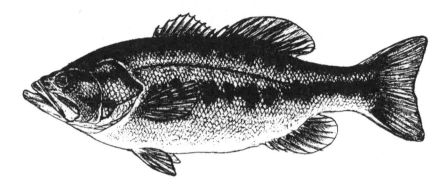

The honest, enthusiastic, unrestrained, wholehearted way that a largemouth wallops a surface lure has endeared him forever to my heart. Nothing that the smallmouth does can compare with the announced strike of his big-mouthed cousin.

JOHN ALDEN KNIGHT
BLACK BASS (1949)

To the tweedy followers of *Salmo salar* and *Salvelinus fontinalis*, such words as "black bass" soured on the tongue like domestic caviar.

PAT SMITH
"OLD IRON JAW"
LAMAR UNDERWOOD'S BASS ALMANAC (1979)

A full moon and a big spangle of stars make a romantic setting, but bass like darkness better. . . . The best fishing usually starts after midnight.

H. G. TAPPLY
THE SPORTSMAN'S NOTEBOOK (1964)

... to master ocean fly fishing, nothing beats *time on the water.*

LOU TABORY
INSHORE FLY FISHING (1992)

———◆———

A trout is vulnerable to the fisherman because he eats.

VINCENT C. MARINARO
IN THE RING OF THE RISE (1976)

———◆———

There are those times when salmon play no part in the proceedings of a day that is ostensibly spent in their pursuit.

DALE REX COMAN
PLEASANT RIVER (1966)

Tail fins, snouts poking out of weedbeds, silver patches where scales are missing against gravels, pinky warts. The more exacting flyfisher looks into the river and asks himself, "When is a trout not a trout." He looks for imaginary trout and takes away the tail, the fins, the gills, the body, the head—hoping something in the tight area he scans holds one or more elements of a trout. Only then can he conclude that a trout is not a trout—when it was never there in the first place.

NEIL PATTERSON
CHALKSTREAM CHRONICLE (1995)

The legend of the trout's sagacity . . . arises from man's conceit. If the trout can outwit us, the lords of creation, he must be superior to us in cunning.

P. B. M. ALLAN
TROUT HERESY (1936)

Trout are quite unaware of their exalted status.

HAROLD BLAISDELL
THE PHILOSOPHICAL FISHERMAN (1969)

. . . when the Trout was opened in the kitchen, within him was found, and sent upstairs to his captor upon a salver, three coppers and a lock ticket.

PATRICK R. CHALMERS
AT THE TAIL OF THE WEIR (1932)

Quite possibly this is the key to fishing: the ability to see glamour in whatever species one may fish for.

HAROLD BLAISDELL
THE PHILOSOPHICAL FISHERMAN (1969)

As to salmon, Walton scarcely speaks a true word about their habits, except by accident.

ANDREW LANG
INTRODUCTION TO WALTON'S *THE COMPLEAT ANGLER* (1906)

Chapter 4

Some Ways
We Do It

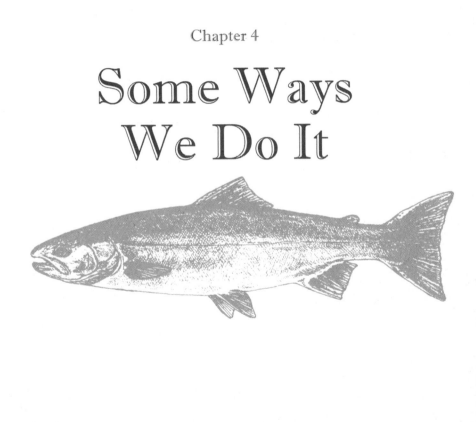

. . . but for the practical part, it is that that makes an Angler; it is diligence, and observation, and practice that must do it.

> Izaak Walton
> *The Compleat Angler* (1653)

. . . left to his own natural instincts and his common sense, any man of reasonable intelligence and sensibility is likely to favor bottom fishing above all other forms.

> Louis D. Rubin Jr.
> *The Even-Tempered Angler* (1983)

To a far greater degree than other kinds of fishing for pleasure, the art of bottom fishing involves the actual catching of fish.

> Louis D. Rubin Jr.
> *The Even-Tempered Angler* (1983)

The art of bottom fishing is that of letting the fish come to the fisherman, instead of vice versa. . . . Bottom fishing, in short, is the Thinking Man's fishing.

LOUIS D. RUBIN JR.
THE EVEN-TEMPERED ANGLER (1983)

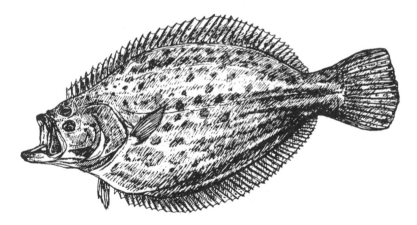

Take along with you a bag, a landing-net and a contented heart. You know the familiar haunts of the perch? Thither go, then.

PATRICK R. CHALMERS
AT THE TAIL OF THE WEIR (1932)

But if you do go ice fishing, do not blame me when you get home, if you do get home. . . . I think that the only important truth I have left out is that a man gets fed up with being comfortable and sane.

ARTHUR R. MACDOUGALL JR.
"FISHING THROUGH THE ICE"
THE TROUT FISHERMAN'S BEDSIDE BOOK (1963)

Ice fishing does offer a maximum of exercise and labor for a minimum of pleasure and excitement.

ARTHUR R. MACDOUGALL JR.
"FISHING THROUGH THE ICE"
THE TROUT FISHERMAN'S BEDSIDE BOOK (1963)

There is no taking trout in dry breeches.

CERVANTES
DON QUIXOTE (1605)

As far as I know, I am the only living human being who has ever caught a fish in the Seine River within the city limits of Paris.

ED ZERN
HOW TO TELL FISH FROM FISHERMEN (1947)

But ah, to fish with a worm, and then not catch your fish! To fail with a fly is no disgrace: your art may have been impeccable, your patience faultless to the end. But the philosophy of worm-fishing is that of results, of having something tangible in your basket when the day's work is done.

BLISS PERRY
FISHING WITH A WORM (1904)

And another thing that makes it easier to ice fish is that one need not worry about his backcasts.

ARTHUR R. MACDOUGALL JR.
"FISHING THROUGH THE ICE"
THE TROUT FISHERMAN'S BEDSIDE BOOK (1963)

The surf: certainly one of nature's finest edges.

RUSSELL CHATHAM
DARK WATERS (1988)

No sport affords a greater field for observation and study than fly fishing, and it is the close attention paid to the minor happenings upon the stream that marks the finished angler.

GEORGE M. L. LA BRANCHE
THE DRY FLY AND FAST WATER (1914)

But we, we locals, detested pier fishing. It meant a crowd; and that meant you lost the chief thing in surfcasting—the luxury of your own solitude.

NEGLEY FARSON
GOING FISHING (1943)

. . . there is no reason whatever why a bottom fisherman cannot enjoy much the same kind of satisfaction as the trout fisherman . . .

LOUIS D. RUBIN JR.
THE EVEN-TEMPERED ANGLER (1983)

On the theory of B. Jarrett Mills, who finds bait fishing more ethical than lure fishing:
The fish, Mills declares, has been made to risk its very existence without any hope of reward.

LOUIS D. RUBIN JR.
THE EVEN-TEMPERED ANGLER (1983)

S: Folks will go to any lengths to catch fish, won't they?
F: Well, yes, Aristotle says that the balletomane skate can easily be caught by a pair of fishermen, using a net if one plays music and the other dances on the deck.

JOHN HERSEY
BLUES (1987)

For this form of fishing [with a wet fly], the rod is no longer a shooting machine but a receiving post, with super-sensitive antennae, capable of registering immediately the slightest reaction of the fish to the fly.

CHARLES RITZ
A FLY FISHER'S LIFE (1959)

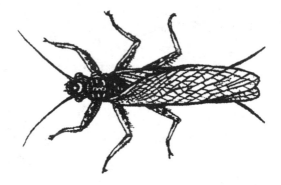

I cannot imagine anybody writing a whole book about maggots, whereas many a man has spent much of his life thinking and writing about fisherman's flies.

ARTHUR RANSOME
THE FISHERMAN'S LIBRARY (1959)

This salt-water fly fishing, it is for men with hard stomachs—like sex after lunch.

CHARLES RITZ
TO ME, AT LUNCH (C. 1972)

You must cultivate an eye for water and an eye for trout. The gift is not easily attained: in all cases it requires practice: and some never acquire it.

JOHN WALLER HILLS
A SUMMER ON THE TEST (1930)

The indications which tell your dry-fly angler when to strike are clear and unmistakable, but those which bid a wet-fly man raise his rod-point and draw in the steel are frequently so subtle, so evanescent and impalpable to the senses, that, when the bending rod assures him that he has divined aright, he feels an ecstasy as though he had performed a miracle each time.

G. E. M. SKUES
MINOR TACTICS OF THE CHALK-STREAM (1910)

Why bother with such as worms, when trout will strike at a floating feather, a red berry, or a pine matchstick.

ARTHUR R. MACDOUGALL JR.
"MATCHSTICKS AND SO ON"
THE TROUT FISHERMAN'S BEDSIDE BOOK (1963)

I continually read of men who said they could be just as happy not catching trout as catching them. To me, that even then sounded pious nonsense, and rather more of an excuse than a statement of fact. . . .

No, I want to get them, and every time I slip on a wader, and put up a fly, it is with this in mind.

BRIAN CLARKE
THE PURSUIT OF THE STILLWATER TROUT (1975)

More voters than anyone thinks would support a Worms-for-Angling ticket. There are worse political slogans.

F. F. VAN DE WATER
IN DEFENSE OF WORMS (1949)

Fly-fishing, may be a very pleasant amusement; but angling, or float-fishing, I can only compare to a stick and a string, with a worm at one end and a fool at the other.

DR. SAMUEL JOHNSON (1709–1784)

That is winter steelheading: long hours of cold, interminable work, punctuated with breathless moments of excitement.

STEVE RAYMOND
THE YEAR OF THE ANGLER (1973)

If I knew all erbout fishin' fer trout, I wu'd give it up and tackle sunthin' more int'resting.

DUD DEAN
VIA ARTHUR R. MACDOUGALL JR. (C. 1949)

. . . the trout and salmon fisherman contrives to make a virtue, a fetish even, of this habitual scarcity, if not entire famine, of catchable fish.

LOUIS D. RUBIN JR.
THE EVEN-TEMPERED ANGLER (1983)

It is the constant—or inconstant—change, the infinite variety in fly-fishing that binds us fast. It is impossible to grow weary of a sport that is never the same on any two days of the year.

THEODORE GORDON (1914)

Chapter 5

When

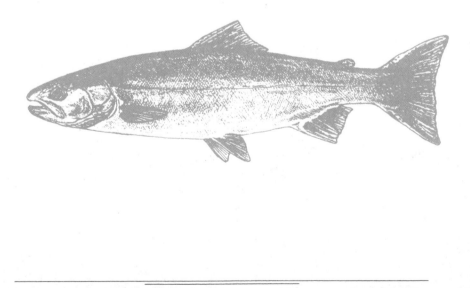

Fishing always reaches its peak at a time when the bugs are thickest. And bugs are thickest at the places where fishing is best. . . . So whenever and wherever you enjoy good fishing you can expect to find mosquitoes, black flies, midges, or deerflies, all lusting for your life's blood.

H.G. TAPPLY
THE SPORTSMAN'S NOTEBOOK (1964)

. . . there are times when flyfishing can seem childishly easy.

TOM SUTCLIFFE, M.D.
REFLECTIONS ON FISHING (1990)

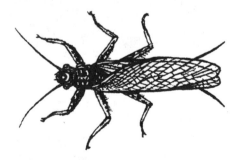

. . . this winter I'm determined for once to fish sensibly, and by that I mean in comfort, to try not only to match the hatch but also to match the weather.

TOM SUTCLIFFE, M.D.
REFLECTIONS ON FISHING (1990)

. . . the good of having wisely invested so much time in wild country . . .

HARRY MIDDLETON
RIVERS OF MEMORY (1993)

. . . you must indure worse luck sometime, or you will never make a good angler.

IZAAK WALTON
THE COMPLEAT ANGLER (1653)

In the Yuan period, the hermit fisherman became the symbol of the unemployed scholar. . . . The true hermit scholar fished for fish, not fame; others merely pretended to fish while waiting to return to politics.

SHENGMU (1310–1360)

There comes a time in every man's life when he is either going to go fishing or do something worse.

HAVILAH BABCOCK
"WHEN A LADY UNDRESSES" (1947)

It mattered little what the weather was, and scarcely more as to the time of year, John Pike must have his fishing every day, and on Sundays he read about it and made flies. All the rest of the time he was thinking about it.

R. D. BLACKMORE (1825–1900)
"CROCKER'S HOLE"

Neek, all I want to do is feesh, feesh, feesh. Everywhere. All the time.

PIERRE AFFRE
TO ME (C. 1985; ALSO 1998)

If fishing interferes with your business, give up your business . . . the trout do not rise in Greenwood Cemetery.

SPARSE GREY HACKLE
"MURDER"
FISHLESS DAYS (1954)

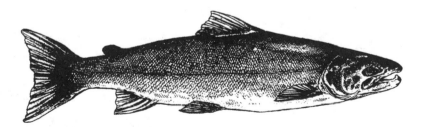

"Then do you mean that I have go to go on catching these damned two-and-a-half pounders at this corner forever and ever?"

The keeper nodded.

"Hell!" said Mr. Castwell.

"Yes," said his keeper.

G. E. M. SKUES
"MR. THEODORE CASTWELL"
SIDELINES, SIDELIGHTS, AND REFLECTIONS (1947)

Chapter 6

Tools and Technical Matters

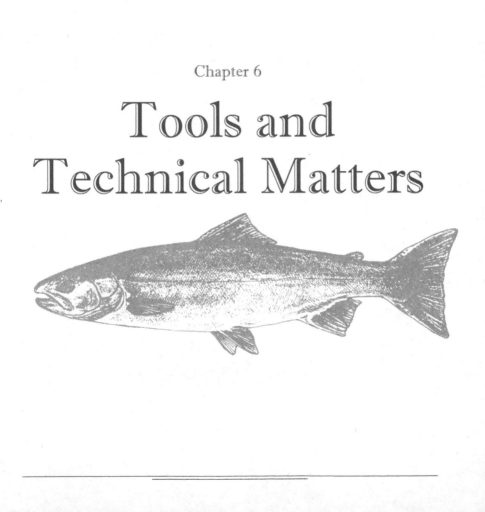

Had all pens that go trout fishing devoted themselves to jotting down notes about why the big fish did not gobble the grasshopper, we should have lost many a page of sunshine, fresh air, and good fellowship, and reaped a crop of fireside Disko troops who thought like the fish.

WILLIAM McFARLAND (1925)

We have been oversold on the short rod.

VINCENT C. MARINARO
IN THE RING OF THE RISE (1976)

I learned how to fly fish in the hit-and-miss, trial-and-error way that makes things stick, and I learned patience, persistence, acceptance and probably a few other good things, too.

JOHN GIERACH
ANOTHER LOUSY DAY IN PARADISE (1996)

Now and then fishermen get excited about a fly that has been "outlawed" in England or the Sahara Desert. That fly is said to be a wicked killer.

ARTHUR R. MACDOUGALL JR.
"THE BEST FLY IS NOT YET"
THE TROUT FISHERMAN'S BEDSIDE BOOK (1963)

The trout fly of today grew out of the trout fly of yesterday.

JOHN MCDONALD
INTRODUCTION TO *THE COMPLETE FLY FISHERMAN* (1947)

... fly tying is the next best thing to fishing; it is the sort of licking of the lips that eases a thirsty man in the desert.

ARTHUR RANSOME
"FLY TYING IN WINTER"
ROD AND LINE (1929)

It is hoped for the roach pole, that it may achieve roaches.

PATRICK R. CHALMERS
AT THE TAIL OF THE WEIR (1932)

The most indispensable item in any fisherman's equipment is his hat. This ancient relic, with its battered crown and well-frayed band, preserves not only the memory of every trout he caught, but also the smell.

COREY FORD
"TOMORROW'S THE DAY" (1952)

One of the few smart things I have ever done was to lay in a last-minute supply of Perfects that will last me my lifetime no matter how cleanly I live.

LEONARD M. WRIGHT JR.
FISHING THE DRY FLY AS A LIVING INSECT (1972)

I know literally thousands of fishermen, yet in all this multitude I can number only four men who can handle a bass fly rod the way it should be handled . . .

JOHN ALDEN KNIGHT
BLACK BASS (1949)

Angling may be said to be so like the mathematics that it can never fully be learnt . . .

IZAAK WALTON
THE COMPLEAT ANGLER (1653)

Fish like an artist and per adventure a good Fish may fall to your share.

CHARLES COTTON
THE COMPLEAT ANGLER (PART 2) (1676)

Learn to identify, and to fish with, the "fly on the water." But do it for the plain, commonsense reason that you are thereby quadrupling your pleasure (to say nothing of rather more than doubling your bag) . . .

J. W. DUNNE
SUNSHINE AND THE DRY FLY (1924)

There is no substitute for fishing sense, and if a man doesn't have it, verily, he may cast like an angel and still use his creel largely to transport sandwiches and beer.

ROBERT TRAVER
TROUT MADNESS (1960)

. . . until man is redeemed he will always take a fly rod too far back . . .

NORMAN MACLEAN
A RIVER RUNS THROUGH IT (1976)

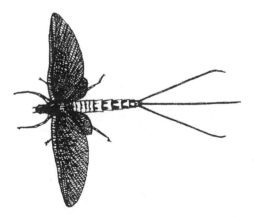

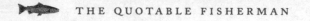

To fish, fine and far off, is the first and principal rule for Trout Angling.

CHARLES COTTON
THE COMPLEAT ANGLER (PART 2) (1676)

. . . there appear to be a few fishermen around who still can't drop a line into a teacup at 50 paces.

H. G. TAPPLY
THE SPORTSMAN'S NOTEBOOK (1964)

The number of people who can throw just sixty feet accurately or inaccurately belong to a regal minority.

VINCENT C. MARINARO
IN THE RING OF THE RISE (1976)

Never throw with a long line when a short one will answer your purpose.

RICHARD PENN (1833)
QUOTED IN *THE ANGLER'S WEEKEND BOOK*, EDITED BY ERIC
TAVERNER AND JOHN MOORE

. . . the things fishermen know about trout aren't facts but articles of faith.

JOHN GIERACH
TROUT BUM (1986)

. . . more big fish are caught within a range of 15 yards than outside it . . .

DERMOT WILSON
FISHING THE DRY FLY (1970)

. . . cast your fly with confidence.

THEODORE GORDON (1914)

I threw a pronounced curve cast and this time when I imparted the minute twitch to the line, the fly moved a sudden inch straight upstream. Then, as it dropped back into a dead drift, it disappeared into the mouth of the best trout of the evening.

LEONARD M. WRIGHT JR.
FISHING THE DRY FLY AS A LIVING INSECT (1972)

Fishing is not like billiards, in which it is possible to attain a disgusting perfection.

ARTHUR RANSOME
"ON GIVING ADVICE TO BEGINNERS"
ROD AND LINE (1929)

Order of Why Trout Take
1. The light-effects of the fly, above and below the surface
2. The way the fly is cast and manipulated, including where the fly is placed relative to the fish
3. Visibility of the leader to the fish
4. The size of the fly
5. Design of the fly
6. Color of the fly
7. Accuracy of imitation of natural insects

EDWARD R. HEWITT
A TROUT AND SALMON FISHERMAN FOR SEVENTY-FIVE YEARS (1948)

Any meticulous attention to color or detail [in a fly pattern] is wasted effort.

VINCENT C. MARINARO
IN THE RING OF THE RISE (1976)

The game [of nods] is played by tying a reasonable fac-simile of the insect being taken by the trout. Then many variations of this basic pattern are tied with only slight differences in each of them. These are in turn cast to a visible feeding trout, and his reaction noted very care-fully. . . . Each fly is cast as long as it receives a nod from the trout. When it no longer excites any nods it is dis-carded for a new variation.

VINCENT C. MARINARO
IN THE RING OF THE RISE (1976)

There is only one secret in dry-fly fishing, which is to make an artificial fly float over a trout in such a way that it looks appetizing enough for him to swallow.

DERMOT WILSON
FISHING THE DRY FLY (1970)

We wish to reproduce as nearly as possible the effect of the insect as it floats upon the stream; to deceive trout that have had enough experience of flies and of fishermen to make them a bit shy and crafty.

THEODORE GORDON (1914)

When dressing dry-flies, we must always keep in mind the fish's point of view rather than our own.

ROMILLY FEDDEN
GOLDEN DAYS (1919)

Just as in cooking there's no such thing as a little garlic, in fishing there's no such thing as a little drag.

H. G. TAPPLY
THE SPORTSMAN'S NOTEBOOK (1964)

Skill at the riverside, or at the fly-table, never came, nor ever will come to us by any road than that of practice.

GEORGE M. KELSON
THE SALMON FLY (1895)

Selectivity is a simple reflex pattern. The cycle of the season is an annual recurrent emergence of insect species, one after another from the river. When each appears it takes a little while before the trout get accustomed to seeing it. Finally they sample the new insect, find it is safe and palatable, and begin to take it regularly.

ERNEST SCHWIEBERT
"TWELVE LESSONS FOR A TROUT-FISHING FRIEND" (1971)

Success begets confidence and confidence begets success—and that fine upward spiral is the best restorative of streamside sanity.

HOWARD T. WALDEN II
UPSTREAM AND DOWN (1938)

Chapter 7

Anglers All

No one under the age of thirty qualifies as a trout bum.

GARY LAFONTAINE
FOREWORD TO *TROUT BUM* BY JOHN GIERACH (1986)

Nothing is more trying to the patience of fishermen than the remark so often made to them by the profane: "I had not patience enough for fishing!"

ARTHUR RANSOME
"FISHERMAN'S PATIENCE"
ROD AND LINE (1929)

. . . a trout fisherman is something that defieth understanding.

COREY FORD AND ALASTAIR MACBAIN
INTRODUCTION TO *TROUT FISHING*
BY DAN HOLLAND (1949)

There are as many reasons why and ways to fish as there are people who do it.

RUSSELL CHATHAM
DARK WATERS (1988)

Do fishermen eat avocados? This is a question no one ever thinks to ask.

RUSSELL CHATHAM
DARK WATERS (1988)

———•••———

Between them, the old men must have created hundreds of trout flies, insect mutants as bizarre and seductive as any ever to drop from a fly tier's vise. With perhaps two exceptions, none of their titillating offerings ever stirred a trout's interest, a fact that didn't bother them at all.

HARRY MIDDLETON
THE EARTH IS ENOUGH (1989)

. . . fishermen constitute a separate class or subrace among the inhabitants of the earth.

GROVER CLEVELAND (1837–1908)

. . . no man is born an artist nor an Angler.

IZAAK WALTON
THE COMPLEAT ANGLER (1653)

We who go a-fishing are a peculiar people. Like other men and women in many respects, we are like one another, and like no others, in other respects. We understand each other's thoughts by an intuition of which we know nothing. We cast our flies on many waters, where memories and fancies and facts rise, and we take them and show them to each other, and small or large, we are content with our catch.

W. C. PRIME
I GO A-FISHING (1873)

There don't have to be a thousand fish in a river; let me locate a good one and I'll get a thousand dreams out of him before I catch him—and, if I catch him, I'll turn him loose.

JIM DEREN, PROPRIETOR
ANGLER'S ROOST

. . . there is great pleasure in being on the sea, in the unknown wild suddeness of a great fish; in his life and death which he lives for you in an hour while your strength is harnessed to his; and there is satisfaction in conquering this thing which rules the sea it lives in.

ERNEST HEMINGWAY
"ON THE BLUE WATER" (C. 1935)

A man can become so caught up in fishing that it actually becomes a grim business . . .

SPARSE GREY HACKLE
"MURDER"
FISHLESS DAYS (1954)

. . . you will search far to find a fisherman to admit that a taste for fishing, like a taste for liquor, must be governed lest it come to possess its possessor . . .

SPARSE GREY HACKLE
"MURDER"
FISHLESS DAYS (1954)

Trigorin, when asked what a great literary man thinks about when he is alone:
I love fishing. I can think of no greater pleasure than to sit alone toward evening by the water and watch a float.

ANTON CHEKHOV
THE SEAGULL (1896)

John Pike was a thick set younker, with a large and bushy head, keen blue eyes that could see through water, and the proper slouch of shoulder into which great anglers ripen . . .

R. D. BLACKMORE (1825–1900)
"CROCKER'S HOLE"

I daresay my friend could cast a fly like an angel, if he put his hand to it; but his mind was on size, nothing else. Huge fish peered at you from every wall of his fine house in London. Dinner conversation was about nothing else. He *was* a fanatic fisherman, so touchy about it that when I tried to rag him that sunset—asking what four flies he had brought up—the beer itself seemed to become soured by his resentment.

NEGLEY FARSON
GOING FISHING (1943)

Arthur Ransome, of W. C. Stewart and Cholmondeley Pennell:
Well, they have both long been dead and, I suppose, fish the Styx, one fishing up and one fishing down and pass each other without speaking.

"RIVALRIES"
ROD AND LINE (1929)

"I hear what you're talking about," said the wife. "But you will make no impression on Humphrey. As long as the fish rise to his bait, everybody is what he ought to be. Bless you, Casaubon has got a trout stream, and does not care about fishing it himself: could there be a better fellow?"

"Well, there is something in that," said the Rector, with his quiet, inward laugh. "It is a very good quality in a man to have a trout stream."

GEORGE ELIOT
MIDDLEMARCH (1871)

I have learned that I am also a person who has to be able to go fishing whenever I can and for as long as I want to go. It is a silly thing, but there it is.

HOWELL RAINES
FLY FISHING THROUGH THE MIDLIFE CRISIS (1993)

The true angler is generally a modest man . . .

THADDEUS NORRIS
THE AMERICAN ANGLER'S BOOK (1864) (BEFORE A BOAST)

Walton without Cotton is like good manners without meat!

ERIC TAVERNER AND JOHN MOORE
THE ANGLER'S WEEKEND BOOK (1949)

. . . just a toast to trout men, one and all. There are so few left, so few who believe the earth is enough.

HARRY MIDDLETON
THE EARTH IS ENOUGH (1989)

About ninety in a hundred fancy themselves anglers. About one in a hundred is an angler.

COL. PETER HAWKER
INSTRUCTIONS TO YOUNG SPORTSMEN (1814)

. . . secretly I lament the hundreds [of fish] we never caught because we forever persisted in fishing only the likeliest holding water.

TOM SUTCLIFFE, M.D.
REFLECTIONS ON FISHING (1990)

. . . impatient sportsmen blame their bad luck.

SERGEI AKSAKOV
NOTES ON FISHING (1847)
TRANSLATED BY THOMAS P. HODGE (1997)

Nick did not like to fish with other men on the river. Unless they were of your party, they spoiled it.

ERNEST HEMINGWAY
"BIG TWO-HEARTED RIVER" (1925)

. . . the dry fly magician, the man who can, with seven ounces of split cane, send a "Tup's indispensible" at the end of four yards of ax gut anywhere, to do, in all conditions, any jiggery-pokery round-the-corner job required of it, is the best of all . . .

PATRICK R. CHALMERS
AT THE TAIL OF THE WEIR (1932)

Chapter 8

A Necessary Passion

La Pêche est ma folie.

Duc de Choiseul (1761)
(quoted by John Waller Hills)

———

It was a long time since Nick had looked into a stream and seen trout. They were very satisfactory.

Ernest Hemingway
"Big Two-Hearted River" (1925)

———

[Fly fishing] is like any other skill, whether it's the knowledge of the Roy Lopez opening in chess, how to hit a golf ball straight, or put spin on a tennis ball, the sheer pleasure of doing something difficult well.

Conrad Voss Bark
A Fly on the Water (1986)

Perhaps all you can say is that there are great lapses or discrepancies in time; that and the simple if inexplicable fact that some people have fishing in their hearts.

RUSSELL CHATHAM
"FISHING: MYSTIQUES AND MISTAKES"
DARK WATERS (1988)

I fish all the time when I'm at home; so when I get a chance to go on vacation, I make sure I get in plenty of fishing.

THOMAS MCGUANE
"FISHING THE BIG HOLE"
AN OUTSIDE CHANCE (1990)

With the exception of painting, nothing in this life has held my interest as much as fishing. Fishing with a fly, bait, a handline; I don't much care. Fishing, in my estimation, is not a hobby, a diversion, a pasttime, a sport, an interest, a challenge, or an escape. It is a necessary passion.

RUSSELL CHATHAM
DARK WATERS (1988)

The outdoor life pleased these old men because they believed any properly obsessed fly fisherman carried rivers and trout inside him.

HARRY MIDDLETON
THE EARTH IS ENOUGH (1989)

If, as I suspect, trout fishing is something of a disease, then it is also something of a therapy in itself.

TOM SUTCLIFFE, M.D.
REFLECTIONS ON FISHING (1990)

I spent the entire dream fishing a single Griffith's gnat.

HARRY MIDDLETON
RIVERS OF MEMORY (1993)

Chapter 9

The Antic Angler

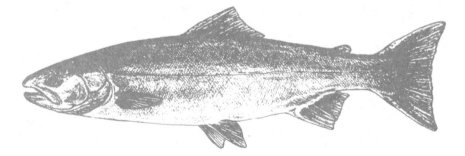

My own experience with the Cleveland Wrecking Yard began two days ago when I heard about a used trout stream they had on sale out at the yard.

RICHARD BRAUTIGAN
TROUT FISHING IN AMERICA (1967)

A Voss Bark Trio

An elderly member of a distinguished fishing club . . . became so bored during the winter closed season that he used to take his fly boxes to bed.

The wife, plucking an errant Blue Charm from a sensitive part of her anatomy, possibly in the dead of night, had a legitimate complaint.

His wife, a good woman at heart, allowed him back into her bed, with his boxes, providing he counted his flies before and after.

CONRAD VOSS BARK
A FLY ON THE WATER (1986)

. . . spending more time with my fly firmly attached to the branches of trees and almost none of it attached to the lips of the trout.

TOM SUTCLIFFE, M.D.
REFLECTIONS ON FISHING (1990)

My mere presence has spoiled the fishing in a half dozen states.

ART SCHECK
WARMWATER FLY FISHING MAGAZINE (1998)

. . . it takes several years of serious fishing before a man learns enough to go through a whole season with an unblemished record of physical and spiritual anguish.

ED ZERN
ARE FISHERMEN PEOPLE? (1951)

On the Firehole I caught thirty-six inches worth of trout—in six installments.

ARNOLD GINGRICH
IN A LETTER TO ME (C.1971)

I waded to shore where I sat and considered the inconsistency of anglers in general and the dumbness of one in particular.

RAY BERGMAN
TROUT (1949)

Like the fish that haunts the angler's dreams, he was forever gaining size.

HARRY MIDDLETON
THE EARTH IS ENOUGH (1989)

There is no use in your walking five miles to fish when you can depend on being just as unsuccessful near home.

MARK TWAIN (1835–1910)

Fishermen are born honest, but they get over it.

ED ZERN
TO HELL WITH FISHING (1945)

A line must always be fastened securely to the inside of the spool. If you forget once and a fish strips the reel naked, you deserve several kicks. If you forget a second time, you are not worth kicking.

ERIC TAVERNER AND JOHN MOORE
"THOUGHTS"
THE ANGLER'S WEEKEND BOOK (1949)

A season does not pass in which I do not find myself misguided by following one of my favourite precepts.

HUISH EDYE
THE ANGLER AND THE TROUT (1945)

I make it a rule never to weigh or measure a fish I've caught, but simply to estimate its dimensions as accurately as possible, and then, when telling about it, to improve those figures by roughly a fifth, or twenty percent. I do this mainly because most people believe all fishermen exaggerate by at least twenty percent, and so I allow for the discounting my audience is almost certain to apply.

ED ZERN
"ARE FISHERMEN REALLY LIARS?" (1977)

A run of fishless days will have me believing that I am hexed, that almost every move I make has some unlucky significance.

HOWARD T. WALDEN II
UPSTREAM AND DOWN (1938)

Under the conditions then prevailing—the thermometer recording 97 degrees in the shade, the stream at its lowest point, and the temperature of the water very high—I really believe that the only chance he might have had would have been with a very "wet" mint julep.

GEORGE M. L. LA BRANCHE
THE DRY FLY AND FAST WATER (1914)

A trout's brain is very small. It is sometimes said that dry-fly fishermen "pit their brains against those of the trout." No-one has ever levelled a bigger insult at us.

DERMOT WILSON
FISHING THE DRY FLY (1970)

The chief difference between big-game fishing and weightlifting is that weightlifters never clutter up their library walls with stuffed barbells.

ED ZERN
HOW TO TELL FISH FROM FISHERMEN (1947)

Most fishing rods work better if you grasp them at the thick end. If you grasp a fisherman at the thick end, you may get a thumb bit off.

ED ZERN
HOW TO TELL FISH FROM FISHERMEN (1947)

To bring to gaff a salmon than a bluefin tuna I would suna.

ED ZERN
HOW TO TELL FISH FROM FISHERMEN (1947)

It is easy to tell tourists from tarpon. Tarpon have a narrow, bony plate inside the mouth on the lower jaw. Tourists (especially in St. Petersburg) have both upper and lower plates.

ED ZERN
HOW TO TELL FISH FROM FISHERMEN (1947)

Fly fishermen are generally well camouflaged. Indeed, some are so well camouflaged that a senior member of the Flyfishers' who fished the Kennet at Chamberhouse had the reputation of being practically indistinguishable from a tree.

CONRAD VOSS BARK
A FLY ON THE WATER (1986)

The truth is, fish have very little sex life. If you have ever tried to make love under water, you will know why.

ED ZERN
HOW TO TELL FISH FROM FISHERMEN (1947)

Contrary to a common belief, it is not true that if you cut a worm-fisherman in half, each half will grow into a complete fisherman. For which we should all be grateful.

ED ZERN
HOW TO TELL FISH FROM FISHERMEN (1947)

The pool was but a stone's throw from the house, and I arrived there in a few minutes, only to find a boy disturbing the water by dredging it with a worm. Him I lured away with a cake of chocolate . . .

GEORGE M. L. LA BRANCHE
THE DRY FLY AND FAST WATER (1914)

Take my friends and my home—as an outcast I'll roam:
　　Take the money I have in the bank: It is just what I
Wish, but deprive me of fish,
　　And my life would indeed be a blank!

LEWIS CARROLL (1832–1895)
"THE TWO BROTHERS"

. . . there are two distinct kinds of visits to tackle-shops, the visit to buy tackle and the visit which may be described as Platonic when, being for some reason unable to fish, we look for an excuse to go in, and waste a tackle dealer's time.

ARTHUR RANSOME
"ON TACKLE SHOPS"
ROD AND LINE (1929)

I never lost a little fish—
Yes, I am free to say.
It always was the biggest fish
    I caught, that got away.

EUGENE FIELD (1850–1895)

Chapter 10

The Essence
of the Pursuit

. . . the tyrannical fascination which angling holds for all those who have once been initiated into its mysteries.

RAFAEL SABATINI (1875–1950)

The take instantly validates our efforts, conferring a measure of definitiveness and closure to an enterprise otherwise riddled with uncertainty and inconclusiveness. Few things in life, I think, have this to offer.

TED LEESON
THE HABIT OF RIVERS (1994)

. . . there is nothing clinical about fishing . . . there is nothing about it that can be viewed in a clinical vacuum. Everything—as in everything else—relates to everything else; and the deeper down one goes, the nearer the quick of life one draws.

BRIAN CLARKE
THE PURSUIT OF THE STILLWATER TROUT (1975)

Fishing is a quest for knowledge and wonder as much as a pursuit of fish; it is as much an acquaintance with beavers, dippers, and other fishermen as it it the challenge of catching trout.

PAUL SCHULLERY
MOUNTAIN TIME (1984)

I fish because I love to; because I love the environs where trout are found, which are invariably beautiful . . . and, finally not because I regard fishing as being so terribly important but because I suspect that so many of the other concerns of men are equally important— and not nearly so much fun.

ROBERT TRAVER
ANATOMY OF A FISHERMAN (1964)

. . . neither time nor repetition has destroyed the illusion that the rise of a trout to a dry fly is properly regarded in the light of a miracle.

HAROLD BLAISDELL
THE PHILOSOPHICAL FISHERMAN (1969)

Perhaps fishing is, for me, only an excuse to be near rivers. If so, I'm glad I thought of it.

RODERICK L. HAIG-BROWN
A RIVER NEVER SLEEPS (1946)

And if ye angler take fysshe; surely thenne is there noo man merier than he is in his spyryte.

DAME JULIANA BERNERS
THE BOKE OF ST. ALBANS (1496)

There is only one theory about angling in which I have perfect confidence, and this is that the two words, least appropriate to any statement, about it, are the words "always" and "never."

LORD GREY OF FALLODON
FLY-FISHING (1899)

Fishing . . . is conducted under continuous tension.

ARTHUR RANSOME
"FISHERMAN'S PATIENCE"
ROD AND LINE (1929)

. . . the sporting qualities of a fish are dependent neither on its size nor its weight, but on the effort of concentration, the skill and mastery it demands from the fisherman.

CHARLES RITZ
A FLY FISHER'S LIFE (1959)

Were it possible to take a limit of trout every time we fished our favorite stream, how long would it take before the sport began to pall?

ART FLICK
ART FLICK'S STREAMSIDE GUIDE (1947)

Fly-fishing is solitary, contemplative, misanthropic, scientific in some hands, poetic in others, and laced with conflicting aesthetic considerations. It is not even clear if catching fish is actually the point.

JOHN GIERACH
DANCES WITH TROUT (1994)

Fly fishing is to fishing as ballet is to walking.

HOWELL RAINES
FLY FISHING THROUGH THE MIDLIFE CRISIS (1993)

I chose my cast, a march brown and a dun,
And ran down to the river, chasing hope.

WILFRED S. BLUNT
A NEW PILGRIMAGE (1889)

Fishing consists of a series of misadventures interspersed by occasional moments of glory.

HOWARD MARSHALL
REFLECTIONS ON A RIVER (1967)

The love of angling increases with the lapse of years, for its love grows by what it feeds on.

> JAMES HENSHALL
> *BOOK OF THE BLACK BASS* (1881)

. . . tis not all of fishing to fish.

> IZAAK WALTON
> *THE COMPLEAT ANGLER* (1653)

The charm of fishing is that it is the pursuit of something that is elusive but attainable, a perpetual series of occasions for hope.

> JOHN BUCHAN (1875–1940)

The music of angling is more compelling to me than anything contrived in the greatest symphony hall.

> A. J. MCCLANE
> "SONG OF THE ANGLER" (1967)

... not everything about fishing is noble and reasonable and sane. ... Fishing is not an escape from life, but often a deeper immersion into it, all of it, the good and the awful, the joyous and the miserable, the comic, the embarrassing, the tragic, and the sorrowful.

HARRY MIDDLETON
RIVERS OF MEMORY (1993)

... the most honest, ingenious, harmless art of Angling.

IZAAK WALTON
THE COMPLEAT ANGLER (1653)

I have learned not to go crazy if I hike for a while only to find someone in my private water.

STEVEN J. MEYERS
SAN JUAN RIVER CHRONICLE (1994)

Calling fishing a hobby is like calling brain surgery a job.

PAUL SCHULLERY
MOUNTAIN TIME (1984)

Only those become weary of angling who bring nothing to it but the idea of catching fish.

RAFAEL SABATINI (1875–1950)

The wildness and adventure that are in fishing still recommend it to me.

HENRY DAVID THOREAU
WALDEN (1854)

A really crushing blow from Fate, such as the loss of three salmon one after the other . . .

H. T. SHERINGHAM
FISHING: ITS CAUSE, TREATMENT, AND CURE (C. 1912)

. . . fishermen value most the fish that are hard to take and value least those that are offered to everybody on a fishmonger's slab.

ARTHUR RANSOME
ROD AND LINE (1929)

I doubt if I shall ever outgrow the excitement bordering on panic which I feel the instant I know I have a strong, unmanageable fish, be it brook trout, brown trout, cutthroat, steelhead, or salmon on my line.

EDWARD WEEKS
FRESH WATERS (1968)

You can't say enough about fishing. Though the sport of kings, it's just what the deadbeat ordered.

THOMAS MCGUANE
IN *SILENT SEASONS*, EDITED BY RUSSELL CHATHAM (1978)

[Angling] is tightly woven in a fabric of moral, social, and philosophical threads which are not easily rent by the violent climate of our times.

A. J. MCCLANE
"SONG OF THE ANGLER" (1967)

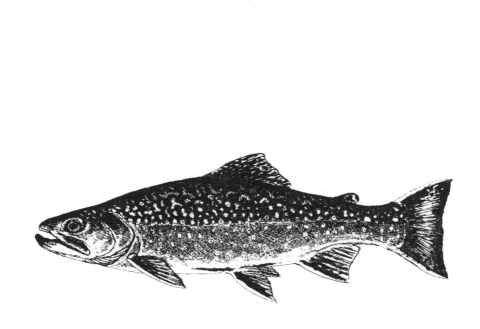

For while the trout fisherman's efforts are ostensibly aimed at taking trout, his preoccupation is concerned with preserving the illusion that his elaborate methodology is at all times justified.

HAROLD BLAISDELL
THE PHILOSOPHICAL FISHERMAN (1969)

My elation at taking that particular fish was quite beyond rational justification. I experienced an illusion of triumph which contained not only the impression that I had finally succeeded in outfoxing a shrewd and calculating adversary, but that the trout had been made to know the humiliation of defeat.

HAROLD BLAISDELL
THE PHILOSOPHICAL FISHERMAN (1969)

. . . so here's to you a hearty draught, and to all that love us, and the honest art of Angling.

IZAAK WALTON
THE COMPLEAT ANGLER (1653)

I still don't know why I fish or why other men fish, except that we like it and it makes us think and feel.

RODERICK L. HAIG-BROWN
A RIVER NEVER SLEEPS (1946)

Certainly no aspect of fly fishing is as enjoyable as those which have a good, firmly based and well established myth or two for company.

CONRAD VOSS BARK
A FLY ON THE WATER (1986)

Fishing textbooks being written by intensely practical men, sometimes omit to remind us, if their authors think of it at all, that fly fishing needs to have a touch of magic about it if we are to enjoy it to the full.

CONRAD VOSS BARK
A FLY ON THE WATER (1986)

Perhaps fishing is, for me, only an excuse to be near rivers.

RODERICK L. HAIG-BROWN
A RIVER NEVER SLEEPS (1946)

. . . there has ever been a delightful uncertainty attending the angler's art, and therein lies one of its chiefest charms.

JAMES HENSHALL
BOOK OF THE BLACK BASS (1881)

We may say of angling as Dr. Boteler said of strawberries:

"Doubtless God could have made a better berry, but doubtless God never did, and so, if I might be judge, God never did make a more calm, quiet, innocent recreation than angling."

IZAAK WALTON
THE COMPLEAT ANGLER (1653)

Chapter 11

Ethical Matters

A man can be a fish hog with a fly rod as easily as he can with a cane pole. Easier perhaps.

H. G. Tapply
The Sportsman's Notebook (1964)

. . . the art of angling, the cruelest, the coldest, the stupidest of pretended sports.

Lord Byron
Note to *Don Juan* (1818)

Angling, too, that solitary vice,
Whatever Izaak Walton sings or says; The quaint, old, cruel coxcomb in his gullet
Should have a hook, and a small trout to pull it.

Lord Byron
Don Juan (1818)

. . . had I a river I would gladly let all honest anglers that use the fly cast line in it, but, where there is no protection, then nets, poison, dynamite, slaughter of fingerlings, and unholy baits devastate the fish, so that 'free fishing' spells no fishing at all.

ANDREW LANG
INTRODUCTION TO WALTON'S *THE COMPLEAT ANGLER* (1906)

I object to fishing tournaments less for what they do to fish than what they do to fishermen.

TED WILLIAMS (1984)

As the old fisherman remarked after explaining the various ways to attach a frog to a hook, it's all the same to the frog.

PAUL SCHULLERY
MOUNTAIN TIME (1984)

. . .the fisherman fishes. It is at once an act of humility and a small rebellion. And it is something more. To him his fishing is an island of reality in a world of dream and shadow.

ROBERT TRAVER
TROUT MADNESS (1960)

Fly-fishing, or any other sport fishing, is an end in itself and not a game or competition among fishermen . . .

ED ZERN
"THE ETHICS, PERHAPS, OF FLY FISHING" (1966)

Catch-and-release fishing is an ecological necessity, not my preference. The practice smacks of bad faith, an inauthentic act.

CHRISTOPHER CAMUTO
"CAUGHT BY THE WAY"
IN PRAISE OF WILD TROUT (1998)

If trout suffer keen anguish while being "played," what do they suffer with? Not with any such brain or nervous system as ours . . .

ODELL SHEPHERD
THY ROD AND THY CREEL (1930)

Game fish are too valuable to be caught only once.

LEE WULFF
LEE WULFF'S HANDBOOK OF FRESHWATER FISHING (1939)

The wildness and adventure that are in fishing still recommend it to me.

HENRY DAVID THOREAU
WALDEN (1854)

Chapter 12

Fisherman's Autumn

. . . next to the pleasure of reading a favourite fishing book comes that of persuading a friend to read it too.

ARTHUR RANSOME
THE FISHERMAN'S LIBRARY (1959)

Fishing, if I a fisher may protest,
Of pleasures is the sweet'st, of sports the best,
Of exercises the most excellent
Of recreations the most innocent.
But now the sport is marde, and wott ye why
Fishes decrease, and fishers multiply.

THOMAS BASTARD (1598)

I carry fewer flies each year, and less gear. Each year I watch a little more, fish a little less. My expertise with a fly rod, such as it is, fails to improve much.

CHRISTOPHER CAMUTO
A FLY FISHERMAN'S BLUE RIDGE (1990)

The ancients wrote of the three ages of man; I
propose to write of the three ages of the fisherman.
When he wants to catch all the fish he can.
When he strives to catch the largest fish.
When he studies to catch the most difficult fish
he can find, requiring the greatest skill and most
refined tackle, caring more for the sport than the fish.

EDWARD R. HEWITT
A TROUT AND SALMON FISHERMAN FOR SEVENTY-FIVE YEARS (1948)

The years will bring their Anodyne,
But I shall never quite forget
The fish that I had counted mine
And lost before they reached the net.

COLIN ELLIS
"THE DEVOUT ANGLER"
QUOTED IN ARTHUR R. MACDOUGALL JR.'S *THE TROUT FISHERMAN'S BEDSIDE BOOK* (1963)

It's just that the longer that I fish, the more I long for simplification and lightness.

TOM SUTCLIFFE, M.D.
REFLECTIONS ON FISHING (1990)

In the recollection of the trout fisherman it is always spring. The blackbird sings of a May morning. The little trout jump in the riffles, and the German brown comes surely to the fly on the evening rise.

R. PALMER BAKER
THE SWEET OF THE YEAR (1965)

Here lies poor Thompson, all alone,
As dead and cold as any stone.
In wading in the river Nith,
He took a cold, which stopp'd his breath.
He fish'd the stream for ten years past,
Death caught him in his net at last.

WRITTEN ON A TOMBSTONE IN DUMPHRIES, ENGLAND.
QUOTED BY TIM BENN IN
THE (ALMOST) COMPLEAT ANGLER (1988)

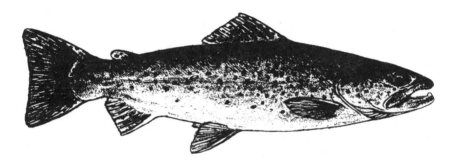

In the autumn, fishing is coming to an end, and each day you are parting with it—for a long time, for a whole six months.

Sergei Aksakov (1791–1859)
"Memoir," translated by Arthur Ransome

Works and Authors Quoted

Pierre Affre (c. 1985)

Sergei Aksakov
Notes on Fishing (1847)
Translated by Thomas P. Hodge (1997)

Sergei Aksakov
"Memoir"
Translated by Arthur Ransome

P. B. M. Allan
Trout Heresy (1936)

Sheridan Anderson
The Curtis Creek Manifesto (1978)

Havilah Babcock
"When a Lady Undresses" (1947)

Stanley M. Babson
Bonefishing (1965)

John Bailey
Reflections on the Water's Edge (N. D.)

R. Palmer Baker
The Sweet of the Year (1965)

Thomas Bastard (1598)

Robert Behnke
"Wild Trout and Native Trout—Is There a Difference?"
In Praise of Wild Trout (1998)

Tim Benn
The (Almost) Compleat Angler (1988)

Ray Bergman
Trout (1949)

Dame Juliana Berners
The Boke of St. Albans (1496)

R. D. Blackmore (1825–1900)
"Crocker's Hole"

Harold Blaisdell
The Philosophical Fisherman (1969)

Wilfred S. Blunt
A New Pilgrimage (1889)

Richard Brautigan
Trout Fishing in America (1967)

John Buchan (1875–1940)

John Bunyan
Pilgrim's Progress (1678)

Lord Byron (1788–1824)
Don Juan (1818)

Christopher Camuto
A Fly Fisherman's Blue Ridge (1990)

Christopher Camuto
"Caught by the Way"
In Praise of Wild Trout (1998)

Lewis Carroll (1832–1895)
"The Two Brothers"

Cervantes
Don Quixote (1605)

Patrick R. Chalmers
At the Tail of the Weir (1932)

Russell Chatham
Dark Waters (1988)

Anton Chekhov
The Seagull (1896)

Duc de Choiseul (1761)

Brian Clarke
The Pursuit of the Stillwater Trout (1975)

Grover Cleveland (1837–1908)

Dale Rex Coman
Pleasant River (1966)

Charles Cotton
The Compleat Angler (Part 2) (1676)

Jim Deren
Proprietor, Angler's Roost
(often quoted)

J. W. Dunne
Sunshine and the Dry Fly (1924)

Huish Edye
The Angler and the Trout (1945)

George Eliot
Middlemarch (1871)

George Eliot
The Mill on the Floss (1860)

Colin Ellis
"The Devout Angler" (N.D.)

John Engels
"Bullhead"
Big Water (1995)

Negley Farson
Going Fishing (1943)

Romilly Fedden
Golden Days (1919)

Eugene Field (1850–1895)

Art Flick
Art Flick's Streamside Guide (1947)

Corey Ford
"Tomorrow's the Day" (1952)

Corey Ford and Alastair MacBain
Introduction to *Trout Fishing* by Dan Holland (1949)

John Gierach
Another Lousy Day in Paradise (1996)

John Gierach
Dances with Trout (1994)

John Gierach
Trout Bum (1986)

Arnold Gingrich (c. 1971)

Theodore Gordon (1914)

John Graves
Goodbye to a River (1960)

Lord Grey of Fallodon
Fly-Fishing (1899)

Sparse Grey Hackle
"Murder"
Fishless Days (1954)

Roderick L. Haig-Brown
A River Never Sleeps (1946)

Col. Peter Hawker
Instructions to Young Sportsmen (1814)

Ernest Hemingway
"Big Two-Hearted River" (1925)

Ernest Hemingway
"Marlin off the Morro" (1933)

Ernest Hemingway
"On the Blue Water" (c. 1935)

James Henshall
  Book of the Black Bass (1881)

W. H. Herbert (Frank Forester)
  Fishes and Fishing (1850)

John Hersey
  Blues (1987)

Edward R. Hewitt
  A Trout and Salmon Fisherman for Seventy-Five Years
  (1948)

John Waller Hills
  A Summer on the Test (1930)

Dr. Samuel Johnson (1709–1784)

J. H. Keene
  The Practical Fisherman (N.D.)

George M. Kelson
  The Salmon Fly (1895)

John Alden Knight
  Black Bass (1949)

George M. L. La Branche
  The Dry Fly and Fast Water (1914)

Gary LaFontaine
  Foreword to *Trout Bum* by John Gierach (1986)

Ben Hur Lampman
  A Leaf from French Eddy (1965)

Andrew Lang
Introduction to *The Compleat Angler* (1906)

Peter Lapsley
River Trout Flyfishing (1988)

Ted Leeson
The Habit of Rivers (1994)

Arthur R. Macdougall Jr.
"Rods and Rods"
The Trout Fisherman's Bedside Book (1963)

Norman Maclean
A River Runs Through It (1976)

Vincent C. Marinaro
In the Ring of the Rise (1976)

Howard Marshall
Reflections on a River (1967)

A. J. McClane
"Song of the Angler" (1967)

John McDonald
Introduction to *The Complete Fly Fisherman* (1947)

William McFarland (1925)

Thomas McGuane
"Fishing the Big Hole"
An Outside Chance (1990)

Thomas McGuane
"Midstream"
An Outside Chance (1990)

Thomas McGuane
in Russell Chatham's *Silent Seasons* (1978)

Steven J. Meyers
San Juan River Chronicle (1994)

Harry Middleton
The Earth Is Enough (1989)

Harry Middleton
Rivers of Memory (1993)

Thaddeus Norris
The American Angler's Book (1864)

Paul O'Neil
"Excalibur: The Steelhead" (1957)

Margot Page
Little Rivers (1995)

Tom Palmer
"Trout Habitat in the Blackfoot Country"
In Praise of Wild Trout (1998)

Neil Patterson
Chalkstream Chronicle (1995)

Richard Penn (1833)

Bliss Perry
Fishing with a Worm (1904)

Roland Pertwee
"The River God" (1928)

W. C. Prime
I Go A-Fishing (1873)

Howell Raines
Fly Fishing through the Midlife Crisis (1993)

Arthur Ransome
The Fisherman's Library (1959)

Arthur Ransome
Rod and Line (1929)

Steve Raymond
The Year of the Angler (1973)

Charles Ritz
A Fly Fisher's Life (1959)

Charles Ritz (c. 1972)

Louis D. Rubin Jr.
The Even-Tempered Angler (1983)

Rafael Sabatini

M. H. "Dutch" Salmon
The Catfish as Metaphor (1997)

Art Scheck
Warmwater Fly Fishing (magazine) (1998)

Paul Schullery
Mountain Time (1984)

Ernest Schwiebert
"Twelve Lessons for a Trout-Fishing Friend" (1971)

Shengmu (1310–60)

Odell Shepherd
Thy Rod and Thy Creel (1930)

H. T. Sheringham
Coarse Fishing (1912)

H. T. Sheringham
Fishing: Its Cause, Treatment, and Cure (c. 1912)

G. E. M. Skues
Minor Tactics of the Chalkstream (1910)

G. E. M. Skues
"Mr. Theodore Castwell"
Sidelines, Sidelights, and Reflections (1947)

Pat Smith
Lamar Underwood's Bass Almanac (1979)

Pat Smith
"Old Iron Jaw"

Tom Sutcliffe, M.D.
Reflections on Fishing (1990)

Lou Tabory
Inshore Fly Fishing (1992)

H. G. Tapply
The Sportsman's Notebook (1964)

Eric Taverner and John Moore
The Angler's Weekend Book (1949)

Leslie P. Thompson
Fishing in New England (1955)

Henry David Thoreau
Walden (1854)

Robert Traver
Anatomy of a Fisherman (1964)

Robert Traver
Trout Madness (1960)

Mark Twain (1835–1910)

F. F. Van de Water
In Defense of Worms (1949)

Conrad Voss Bark
A Fly on the Water (1986)

Howard T. Walden II
Upstream and Down (1938)

Izaak Walton
The Compleat Angler (1653)

Edward Weeks
Fresh Waters (1968)

Hewitt Wheatly
The Rod and Line (1847)

Ted Williams (1984)

Dermot Wilson
Fishing the Dry Fly (1970)

Leonard M. Wright Jr.
Fishing the Dry Fly as a Living Insect (1972)

Joan Wulff
Fly Casting Techniques (1987)

Lee Wulff
Lee Wulff's Handbook of Freshwater Fishing (1939)

Ed Zern
Are Fisherman People? (1951)

Ed Zern
"Are Fishermen Really Liars?" (1977)

Ed Zern
"The Ethics, Perhaps, of Fly Fishing" (1966)

Ed Zern
How to Tell Fish from Fishermen (1947)

Ed Zern
To Hell with Fishing (1945)

Some Very Personal Notes
on Some of the Authors

Pierre Affre is one of the world's great fishermen—a tournament caster with fly rod, spinning rod, and bait-casting equipment—but an even greater enthusiast for fishing itself. He lives in the heart of Paris, with tarpon scales the size of pancakes tacked to the door of his office and his equipment ready at every moment for a trip to Oregon, Senegal, Iceland, Russia, the Florida Keys, a Scottish salmon river, or wherever he can find sport. On a recent visit he told me there was "fantas-teek" fishing in the Seine, below Pont Neuf, a few hundred yards from his aparment, for catfish.

Sergei Aksakov, the great Russian memoirist and Leo Tolstoy's favorite writer, is far too little known by English-speaking anglers. He was a passionate angler and we must be hugely grateful for Thomas Hodge's recent translation of *Notes on Fishing* and Arthur Ransome's earlier translations.

Sheridan Anderson was a huge man, I'm told, and sometimes wore a cape. His wonderful *Curtis Creek Manifesto* should be required reading for all new fly fishers. He's independent, original, shrewdly focused on what we really need to know. How I wish I'd known him.

R. Palmer Baker is a close friend and a superb fly fisher. He's the "sweetest" of men in all the best connotations of that word—kindly, interested in others, warm, and generous. I only wish I fished with him—and others like him—more often.

Robert Behnke is our great trout biologist—the arbiter and authority on technical matters. Between reading Bob's work and that of Bill Willers, you'll know enough to "think like a trout," if that's what you really want to do.

Timothy Benn founded my little book-publishing business, as a subsidiary of Ernest Benn Ltd., an old English publisher. He is hugely generous and exuberant—and the few times we fished together he worked magic with a fly rod.

Ray Bergman is the most sensible and respected angler-writer of the mid-twentieth century. His *Trout* is the book we all read—and it is still one of the best all-around books on the subject.

Dame Juliana Berners is still something of an enigma to us, and her book (which I readily agree she wrote) is the heart of John McDonald's *The Origins of Angling*—and still immensely readable. Her no-hackle flies, from the fifteenth century, are remarkably akin to some recent no-hackles.

R. D. Blackmore wrote the famous novel *Lorna Doone*, which I can't read. His "Crocker's Hole," though, is one of my great favorites.

Harold Blaisdell had one of those enviably modest and practical minds; his *Philosophical Fisherman* and *Tricks that Take Fish* are models of sensible, down-to-earth, and genuinely helpful writing about fishing.

Richard Brautigan's *Trout Fishing in America* is remarkably like nothing else you've read—and only fleetingly (and brilliantly) about trout fishing.

John Buchan was John F. Kennedy's favorite author—though not because of his writing about fishing. Buchan's *The Thirty-nine Steps* made a marvelous movie—though there's no fishing in it.

Lord Byron hated fishing—and I don't. He still seems a good stay on all my rampant enthusiasm for the sport.

Christopher Camuto is one of the finest younger writers on fly fishing working today. His *Fly Fisherman's Blue Ridge* is a gem.

Russell Chatham is chiefly known today as a painter—and his paintings are superb. But he's a first-rate writer and I wish we'd see more words from him, too.

Brian Clarke introduced me to the Kennet and (with John Goddard, in *The Trout and the Fly*) to new ways of viewing trout fishing. He's been the Angling Correspondent for the *London Times* for many years.

Jim Deren was the legendary proprietor of The Angler's Roost in New York City's Chrysler Building. Ian Frazier did a brilliant profile of him in *The New Yorker*, which you can find in *Nobody Better, Better Than Nobody*. Deren once asked Neil Patterson if Neil had ever seen flies as small as those in his hand. Deren's hand was empty.

George Eliot. Isn't it good that major literary figures have interesting things to say about fishing now and then?

John Engels is primarily a poet who loves to fish—but when he tells me that fishing is the "one coherent passion" in his life, I worry that he's a fisherman who also writes poetry.

Negley Farson's *Going Fishing* is one of a dozen books every fisherman should read. It radiates passion for exploration—and the sport.

Romilly Fedden was a painter living in France just before World War I. His *Golden Days*, one of my favorite books, is poignant and heartfelt.

Art Flick's *Streamside Guide* was the first fishing book I published; it's still in print thirty years later, and fifty years after Art wrote it. Despite all that's been published since, his earthy approach to entomology is still the best introduction to trout-stream bugs and how they behave. We spent many good days together on his Schoharie.

John Gierach is our most popular fly-fishing writer today—and a great treasure. Behind his laid-back nonchalance, you'll find enviable skill and art. We once had a terrific day on the Gallatin not-catching fish.

Arnold Gingrich used to get up at 4:00 A.M., fish the Joe Jefferson Club ponds in all seasons, take the bus to New York City and practice the violin at Wurlitzer, and then arrive at his office at *Esquire* magazine before 7:30. When I was editing his *Joys of Trout*, he frequently called me that early. Once he fell asleep at lunch—but picked up the conversation without missing a beat. A great man—and a great lover of fly fishing.

Theodore Gordon is still the subject of much debate—and much difference of opinion. He's called "patron saint," "father of fly fishing," and overrated recluse. I tend to take John McDonald's view that we should read the man and he will tell us all we need to know.

John Graves is one of the finest writers in America—careful, wise, without the capacity (from all I can tell) to write a false word. His home is a hard-scrabble farm in Texas and he has made of it and his world the most memorable prose. He introduced me to tarpon fishing, and I wish only that we'd fished more together.

Sparse Grey Hackle was a great friend, and I have missed our conversation and correspondence sorely since he died more than a decade ago. He had been debating champion of New York State soon after the turn of the century, and always praised his high-school English teacher. He was friend to Edward Hewitt, Harry Darbee, and dozens of other angling legends.

Roderick Haig-Brown is a modern titan—and his book *A River Never Sleeps* remains one of the finest memoirs ever.

Ernest Hemingway. No writer has spawned more imitations or more commentary. I fished his Fox River, the prototype for his "Big Two-Hearted River," several years ago and caught barely a fish.

George M. Kelson says that one shouldn't write about salmon fishing until he's caught 3,000 salmon. If that were a true requirement (for any species) the amount of writing about fishing would be cut by 95 percent.

Ted Leeson is surely one of the finest writers—and fly fishers— of our time. He lives in Corvallis, Oregon, and though he's an English professor, there's nothing academic about his prose.

A. J. McClane's towering *Encyclopedia*, and his many articles in *Field & Stream* and elsewhere, established him as the most knowledgeable angler-writer of our time.

John McDonald ran the mimeograph machine for Leon Trotsky in Mexico City in the 1930s, traveled to Montana with Dan Bailey a few years later, became a writer for *Fortune* magazine, wrote Alfred P. Sloan's *My Years with G. M.* (called the best book on business by Bill Gates), three important angling books, and one of the best books on poker. He's in his nineties and still writing.

Thomas McGuane, a passionate salt- and freshwater fisherman, is one of America's finest novelists.

Norman Maclean's great book was made into "the movie" and probably sent a few million folks to the rivers. Don't blame him for this. His book is a miracle and should be read once a year.

Vincent C. Marinaro is our most intense modern student of the dry fly. He was a crusty fellow who was deeply disappointed when the first edition of *A Modern Dry-Fly Code* sold under 1,000 copies. That edition is a collector's prize now—and subsequent editions have sold more than 35,000 copies.

Steven Meyers is a transplanted New Jerseyite who now lives in Durango, Colorado, and guides on the San Juan. He's not only a fine writer but also a superb photographer.

Harry Middleton was one of our great treasures and his few books were only the beginning of what he might have written. He died of a massive heart attack in his forties—not long after the publication of his last book, written when he was experiencing hard times. His last letters to me are among the most sad and poignant letters I've ever read.

Paul O'Neil, a *Life* magazine writer, wrote too little about fishing. His long essay, *In Praise of Trout and Also Me,* was recently published as a small book. It's about the Esopus and the fishing passion—and it's a gem.

Margot Page, Sparse's granddaughter, learned to fly cast with a Fly-O while she was working with me in a large office loft. She got to doing it pretty well—and writing darn well about it.

Neil Patterson and I can't remember whether he or I said that fishing books should ooze from a riverbank, not rocket out of publishers' offices in big cities. His *Chalkstream Chronicles* is the best evidence that he knew full well what the assertion means. I hope to get closer to those words myself someday.

Roland Pertwee. Be sure to read all of "The River God," one of my favorite stories, and also his perfectly delicious *Fish Are Such Liars*; both were recommended to me by Sparse Grey Hackle.

Steve Raymond's books are always among the most thoughtful writings about fly fishing. He has also been one of our sturdiest and most demanding critics.

Charles Ritz was Pierre Affre's mentor, Gingrich's close friend. I met him only once, with Gingrich, for lunch at Amalfi; he was quite mesmerizing. Except for Pierre, I've never met a greater fishing enthusiast.

Louis D. Rubin is a distinguished English professor, now retired. I've seen him fish with top-water lures but he has cunningly built a theory to defend his passion for bottom fishing.

Art Scheck is editor of *American Angler*. He's from New Jersey but lives in Vermont, where he prefers bass to trout, solid prose to words that creak.

Paul Schullery, Park Historian at Yellowstone National Park, writes equally well about bears and trout and tourists.

Ernest Schwiebert's *Matching the Hatch* was written while he was still a student in college. He is a consummate angler and one of the most widely read of all modern fishermen—and the most international.

Odell Shepherd won a Pulitzer Prize for his superb biography of Bronson Alcott (Louisa May's father—and an innovative teacher). His book *Thy Rod and Thy Creel* has remained one of those neglected classics, possibly because of its dreadful title.

G. E. M. Skues is one of the towering figures in modern angling literature—ever-inquiring, highly literate, the father of whole schools of thought.

Tom Sutcliffe is a South African doctor and a passionate fisher-man. I wish he were better known here, but his book is available only in his own country. Perhaps the quotes here will whet some interest in this fine and thoughtful man.

Lou Tabory is a down-to-earth—and highly innovative—striped-bass addict. His dictum that we can't understand much about our quarry unless we spend *time on the water* is surely correct. I only wish I could.

H. G. "Tap" Tapply has been a fountain of good practical sense to me since I first read his "Tap's Tips" column in *Field & Stream* more than fifty years ago. He's a superb teacher—even when his students have (like me) three thumbs.

Henry David Thoreau fished now and then, was excited by the drama of it—and then appears to have given it up. I never will.

Leslie P. Thompson. How I wish I knew this gentle and witty man—a delightful writer, on everything from trout to carp, and a fine artist. His line drawings can be found in *Art Flick's Streamside Guide*. Art told me he used to chill natural insects and make his paintings of them at the old West Kill Tavern. His chapter on carp fishing is must reading.

Robert Traver's "Testament of a Fisherman" remains one of the most genial and true statements of why we fish and where fishing stands in some larger scheme of things. Quite high is

where. He brought the wisdom of a truly great jurist to his writing, and a novelist's storytelling gifts to his fishing books. A great man—and perfectly unique.

Conrad Voss Bark was the first BBC Parliamentary Correspondent and for many years served as Angling Correspondent to the *London Times*. He lives in Devon, where his wife, Anne, runs the famous Arundell Arms—but he has fished with passion throughout the world.

Howard Walden's *Upstream and Down* was one of the first fishing books I read. Its early sections, on how a boy can get hooked on fishing, still offer one of the finest images of how many of us came to fishing.

Izaak Walton is Izaak Walton.

Edward Weeks, for many years editor and columnist for *The Atlantic Monthly*, loved fishing and wrote wisely about it. I wish he'd written more.

Dermot Wilson once took me and my son Tony to a stretch of the Test and when Tony—then twelve—grew restless, told him to lower a nymph directly to the bottom, count to ten, then jerk upward. The result was a four-pound brown with a huge hooked jaw. Dermot wrote one of the finest basic books on dry-fly fishing.

Leonard M. Wright is a maverick, independent thinker about fishing matters. He promotes ten-foot rods, the "sudden inch," and thinking for yourself.

Joan Wulff was a tournament caster who would have been a national star in any field other than fishing. Happily, she's written three books and shared her techniques on a new video. Everyone who fishes can learn from her.

Lee Wulff was one of the great pioneers in modern fishing—the author of seminal books on salmon fishing, fly tying, and much more. He once told me that he'd scouted for new salmon rivers in Newfoundland by buzzing the rivers in his "Yellow Bird"—dangerous stuff. He was a great teacher and a great conservationist. Lee died in a plane crash, in his eighties.

Ed Zern is the one great angling humorist. I read him when I was a teenager and was happy to publish his last book. He was—as many great humorists are—a very serious man on serious matters, like the ethics of fishing, conservation, the spirit of the sport, and writing exactly the proper sentence. When he had Parkinson's Disease, which eventually killed him, he told me that he didn't mind his hand shaking so much; it improved his "S" cast.

Having finished these notes, and in fact this book, I suddenly realize how many golden words I've left out—from the authors already represented, from dozens of my favorite books, from great writers and fishermen like Austin Francis, Philip Wylie, Dave Whitlock, John Cole, Dave Hughes, Flip Pallot, W. D. Wetherell, Datus Proper, Darrel Martin, John Barsness, Lefty Kreh, and many others. Lefty in particular is quotable at *book* length—although his infectious ebullience is diminished when he doesn't say it himself. Perhaps, after all, there's room for another book; in fact, you can start one in the blank pages that follow the index.

Index